SCHOLASTIC

D1430536

Classroom Fitness Breaks to Help
KIDS
FOCUS

Sarah Longhi

This copy belongs to:
Dr. Sharon Smith

New York • Toronto • London • Auckland • Sydney **Teaching**
Mexico City • New Delhi • Hong Kong • Buenos Aires *Resources*

**To the staff and students at Groove With Me for encouraging my
Kid-Fit program and helping to make this book possible. Dance on!**

*Special thanks to Adam Hyman and his students at PS 101 in New York City, students in my
Kid-Fit classes, Erin Glass Martin for her inspired teaching and enthusiastic support of my
work, and the amazing team of editors and designers who brought their creative vision to this
project—Melinda Belter, Maria Chang, Brian LaRossa, Maria Lilja, and Jaime Lucero. And to
Roger Essley for his innovative stick-figure concept.*

*With deepest gratitude to my movement-education mentors, including Nia founders Debbie
Rosas and Carlos AyaRosas, Susan Hitzmann, Jayne Mielo, and Winalee Zeeb. A special call-
out to Helen Terry, who was the first to show me that fitness can really be fun, and Caroline
Kohles, who helped me shape my fitness work with children.*

Safety Warning! Before using the activities in this book with students, be sure to check
students' health records and/or consult with parents directly to make sure that students have
no physical conditions that would make participating in these activities unsafe for them. If
necessary, seek advice from the school nurse or another licensed medical professional.

Edited by Maria L. Chang
Cover design by Jorge J. Namerow
Interior design by Melinda Belter
Illustrations by Brian LaRossa
Photographs by Maria Lilja

ISBN: 978-0-545-16877-9
Copyright © 2011 by Sarah Longhi.
All rights reserved. Printed in the U.S.A.

   5 6 7 8 9 10   40   18 17 16 15 14 13 12

Contents

*It is exercise alone that supports the spirits,
and keeps the mind in vigor.*

−Cicero (c. 65 BC)

The benefits of fitness have been heralded for centuries. While we can dispute Cicero's claim (certainly, exercise is not the only thing that keeps our spirits up and our minds active), we have strong evidence from recent neurological research that physical fitness can help our minds grow stronger and increase our ability to deal effectively with life's daily stresses. In fact, studies linking students' physical fitness to brain function, learning readiness, and emotional well-being (Ratey, 2008) present new evidence that developmentally appropriate physical activity can change the chemistry and function of the brain in ways that support academic achievement and a positive attitude toward school.

Why Include Physical Activity in the School Day?

Unfortunately, today's students are faced with a number of obstacles to physical activity—from an increasingly sedentary lifestyle to limited opportunities for physical education and recess at school. One surefire way to motivate students and prime their brains for learning during the school day is to get them moving— even for short periods of time—between or during seated tasks.

The activities in this collection provide a jump start for daily fitness at school: They target all areas of fitness—from postural strength to cardiovascular health. Easily adapted to any schedule, they can be used to supplement PE classes and recesses and provide physical breaks during class and in after-school programs.

AUTHOR'S NOTE

This collection of fitness breaks stems from my work as a classroom teacher and as a creative-movement teacher. In the classroom, many of the lessons I developed to reach my diverse group of third and fourth graders included kinesthetically based activities, like Arm-to-Arm Estimation (the Math Bonus on page 12)—these movement activities motivated students to get involved while helping them internalize concepts through physical actions. I've also drawn upon games my colleagues and I developed for recess and after-school programs to target students who had few opportunities to play vigorous games and team sports outside of school.

My continuing work teaching creative movement uses a "minds-on movement" approach based on my training in Nia, a technique that blends martial arts, dance, and yoga in a dynamic way to challenge body and mind together. This approach helps kids enjoy fitness, seek daily movement challenges on their own, work collaboratively with peers, and sharpen their problem-solving skills. I hope you and your students use these exercises as a jumping-off point for more fitness fun and focused learning!

About This Resource

The 50+ fitness breaks in this book are organized by times during the school day when your students need help focusing their attention, releasing stress, and positively channeling their naturally abundant energy. You'll find activities for seated and independent work, walking and waiting in the halls, and recess.

To show you how each activity supports students' fitness, activities are labeled with the key areas of functional fitness they target. These areas—strength, flexibility, mobility, stability, agility, and coordination—are components of a well-rounded fitness program. By doing two or more activities each day, you're sure to help students achieve a balance of movement throughout the week.

Each exercise set comes with easy-to-follow directions, tips for modifications, and step-by-step illustrations. The exercises in Section 2 are written to be displayed on-screen to guide the whole class or to photocopy for independent use at a center or at recess. *Bonus!* curriculum connection tips throughout the book show you how to integrate kinesthetic learning into reading, vocabulary, math, and more.

How to Use This Resource

1. Get started by giving students a couple of fun physical mini-challenges, such as "How many jumping jacks do you think you can do in one minute?" or "How long do you think you can balance on one foot?"

Time students and have them compare their work to their estimate. Have them discuss what they've experienced—for example, getting warmer, feeling their heart beat strongly and their muscles contract, experiencing some wobbling and adjusting while they balance, and having to concentrate on their physical effort. Discuss with students how moving more often can help their bodies and minds work better. Tell them that they'll be learning new fitness warm-ups and games to do throughout the day to help their minds get focused and bodies stay healthy.

Math Mini-Challenge: To explore how physical skills improve with practice and to review estimating and time measurement, try the same mini-challenges each day for a week, timing students (or having them time themselves), then have students revise their estimates. Graph the results—are they noticing that they can do more jumping jacks in the same period of time or hold their balance a second or two longer?

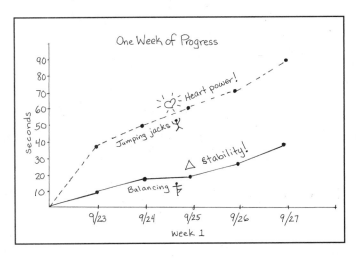

Use an analog clock with a second hand, a free online stopwatch, or a stopwatch tool on the interactive whiteboard to time students.

2. Review Section 1: Moves to Get Started (page 9) and choose activities to help students gain an awareness of the basics of fitness (the Super 6, page 13) and how to do any movement activity safely.

3. Select activities from the rest of the collection to use at different times during your day. The activities can be done separately or combined in any order, so it's easy to integrate them into your schedule, regardless of your daily plan.

4. Involve students as much as possible in selecting and planning their fitness breaks, so they begin to "own" the exercises and contribute their own ideas. A great way to get students who really need to move focused and motivated throughout the day is to assign them as Warm-Up Pros, who learn the exercises or games ahead of time and help demonstrate them to the class.

The activity steps in Section 2: Energizing Breaks for the Classroom are written at a third-grade level; younger students may need you to read the steps aloud, while older students may read the steps with little or no support from you, depending on their reading level.

A Warm-Up Pro leads the activity.

5. Once students have learned an exercise, add the activity to a list of fitness breaks to repeat at a warm-up center or corner of the room. Hang the attached full-color poster in this area to remind them of the key elements of fitness and provide some full-color exercises.

Display Section 2 activities on screen to help students practice reading for a purpose and following directions.

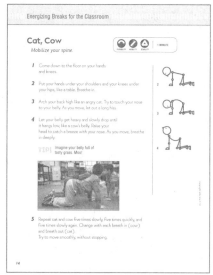

Options for Tight Schedules

Chances are, you're concerned about finding time in your schedule for fitness breaks. Here are some ideas for using the exercises flexibly in a way that supports students' ability to recharge for more concentrated learning.

1-minute transition-time moves: Use a fitness break during any short transition time. Help students refocus and reduce fatigue by offering a single exercise from sections 2 or 3 (classroom and hallway moves).

5-minute brain-break moves: Help students prepare for or recover from a longer seated activity by combining several exercises from sections 2 or 3 or by repeating a single exercise a few times.

15-minute indoor recess: Even a short but vigorous recess can help provide part of the daily sustained exercise time kids need to stay fit and healthy (see following page). In a limited indoor space, you can keep students engaged and challenged by mixing and matching activities from Section 2, adding moves you and your students are familiar with (e.g., jumping jacks), and inviting students to teach the class new moves. A 15-minute indoor exercise in limited space might look like this:

- 1 minute jogging in place
- 1 minute Sit Down, Stand Up—No Hands! (page 34)
- 1 minute jumping jacks
- 1 minute Spread Your Wings (page 39)
- 1 minute In, Forward, Up . . . Down, Back, Out! (page 23)
- Repeat the sequence two more times.

15-minute-or-longer outdoor recess and before-and after-school programs: Select from the action-packed relays, tag variations, and other group games in Section 4. The more time you allot, the greater the impact on students' overall health. (See ideas for integrating more physical activity into the day in the box on page 8.)

TIP! Encourage older students to work in teams to develop 5-minute exercise combinations. Have teams write their combination on chart paper. Pull out one or more team combinations any time your class can take a 5-minute or longer indoor break.

NOTE: Please avoid denying recess as a punishment! Kids who act out usually need recess the most.

MAKING SURE KIDS GET ENOUGH EXERCISE

The U.S. Department of Health and Human Services recommends that children engage in 60 minutes or more of moderate to intense physical activity each day (2008). The good news for limited recess periods is that shorter bursts of physical activity (15–20 minutes) can improve students' cardiovascular health and enhance brain function, and can contribute to the 60-minute daily goal.

If you and your colleagues are working to make fitness a top priority for your students, here are some ways to help.

Take advantage of any recess time available—and see if aides or parent volunteers can help you—to lead the group games that really get kids moving (see Section 4, page 52), or let students choose a variety of high-intensity activities such as running and racing, jumping rope, playing on a jungle gym, and, for older students, tag football, soccer, or basketball. Aim for 15 minutes or more each day, either outdoors or in an open space indoors.

In a limited space for indoor recess, create variations on a routine of activities from Section 2 (see the 15-minute combination on page 7).

With the help of parent and community volunteers or with colleagues, begin an after-school fitness club where kids spend 45 minutes or more playing sports and other vigorous games and then come in for tutorials or to complete homework. Note that their brains will be primed to absorb and process more information after a vigorous workout—post-workout is a great time to work with students who need extra academic help (Ratey, 2008)!

For students who need more exercise opportunities or have trouble focusing in the morning, begin an early-bird fitness club that meets 15 minutes or more before school starts and plan vigorous activities for the type of space you'll be using (see above).

Work with the school nurse and PE teacher to keep parents informed about healthy choices for lunches and snacks and helping their children get adequate daily exercise.

ADVOCATING FOR DAILY RECESS

In addition to engaging in structured physical activities like the ones in this book, children also need unstructured playtime every day—and we can ensure they get it at recess. Some points you may want to present to colleagues, parents, and administrators to promote daily recess include:

- Recess can contribute to the 60 minutes of moderate to vigorous exercise recommended for children each day.

- A 15-minute or longer recess during the school day is associated with improved classroom behavior (Barros et al., 2009).

- Unstructured play at recess is essential for promoting emotional, social, and cognitive growth (Ginsburg et al., 2009).

- Kids literally think and behave better when they've played with other kids!

These activities introduce key concepts students will use in the warm-ups and games in the rest of this collection—the importance of keeping our movements safe and friendly and the benefits and basics of fitness.

KEEPING IT SAFE AND FRIENDLY

Before you ask students to engage in physical activity, they must develop an awareness of how much space they have around them to move safely (without bumping into walls, furniture, or their neighbors). We call this **self space**. They also must understand that when they work together physically, they need to make their contact safe and as gentle as possible. We call this **community space**. Students build self-regulation skills when they practice moving with an awareness of both types of space.

The mini-challenges in this section are a fun way to get kids used to moving mindfully in a variety of spaces with different constraints. Do these mini-challenges as an introduction to the other activities in this book and revisit them as a transition between lessons or other tasks and as a helpful reminder before fast-paced group activities.

CUES TO HELP STUDENTS MOVE MINDFULLY

Keep your self-space.

Is this a community-space or self-space exercise?

How can you help keep your neighbors safe when you do this move?

Check out the space around you. How can you change your position to work in the space better?

Find a spot with enough space to . . . [provide a physical cue related to the warm-up or game].

To keep vigorous group activities like Capture the Ball (page 53) safe and fun, students must practice moving safely—alone and together.

Desk Space Cadets

Students suspend their hands and feet "in self space" while seated at their desks to gain spatial awareness and improve balance and core strength.

1. Ask, "How far and in which directions can you move your arms without touching any neighbors? Your legs?" Let students experiment in self space.

2. Have students hold a pose and then count down from 10. Then, tell them to relax, and have a few volunteers show their innovative positions. Invite everyone to try one of these positions or a new one of their own.

3. Repeat this activity over the next few days or weeks, having students hold a pose for an increasingly longer period of time to increase their core strength and control.

MODIFY! For students with less core strength or balance issues, have them begin by suspending two limbs and keeping two grounded (e.g., float the left foot and right hand only).

My Space Bubble

Working with an imaginary bubble around them, students gain an appreciation of how they must change the way they move depending on the amount of space around them.

1. Have students start this exercise standing away from classmates and furniture. Say, "Imagine you are inside a bubble that surrounds and protects you. Let your hands reach out and feel the entire inside of the bubble, above your head and all around you. Let your feet feel the space all around your legs. This is your biggest self space."

2. Ask students to continue feeling the size of the bubble around them as they move gradually closer to either the center of the room or others in their group. Have them

stop at least twice to reevaluate their self space by feeling the inside of their increasingly smaller "bubble." Bring students close enough to almost touch. Discuss how their self space has changed.

3. Review with students the ways they adjusted to give their peers and themselves room (e.g., pulling their arms and legs closer to their bodies, turning sideways, ducking, etc.). Ask how they can use what they've learned in other group exercises and games.

Mind Our Line

This is a great way to help students use their own physical estimations to move responsibly when they are close to others.

1. Have students line up in the hallway and stand as close as they can to the person in front of them without touching. Ask for students' responses to these questions:

   • What would happen if we moved like this down the hall?

   • How close is too close?

   • How much space is enough to give you time to react to what the person in front of you does?

Using an arm's length between students usually provides enough room for the hallway warm-ups in Section 3.

2. Establish a comfortable distance for walking and a slightly bigger space for doing exercises in the hallways.

MODIFY! Younger students generally need more room to anticipate sudden stops and to make adjustments.

VIGOROUS BUT QUIET APPLAUSE!

Invite your class to invent ways to silently show their appreciation. Here are a few that both release energy and focus attention.
   • Flick hands high and low
   • Clap vigorously without touching palms
   • Pump fists in patterns (e.g., right, right, left, left . . .)

Class Web

The Class Web helps build classroom community as well as space awareness. Try this in the gym, an empty hallway, or outside—and bring your camera.

1. In the center of an open space with a clean, flat surface, invite one student to lie faceup on the ground with arms and legs stretching out to the sides, so he or she looks like a giant starfish.

2. Choose volunteers to build off the first student, gently touching in one or two places: hand to hand, foot to foot, hand to foot, or foot to hand, keeping their limbs stretched long.

3. As more students join the web, challenge them to try to touch at least two different people and encourage the group to help the newcomers find open hands or feet to connect with. Remind them, "As you each find a way to join the web, make your connections gentle."

This amazing web shows "we are all connected." Take a photo for open house displays, writing prompts, and the class memory book.

4. When all students have joined the web, ask them, "What would happen to the web if you could only touch elbows and knees?" (It would get smaller and tighter.) Have them adjust their positions to try to make a new web.

MODIFY! Make a 3-D web by having students connect hands and feet in a web while standing.

Math Bonus! Have students estimate and then measure their own arm span. Older students may estimate the distance across the web and then use a long length of string to find the exact measurement for comparison.

Arm-to-arm estimation

INTRODUCING THE SUPER 6

As you begin trying out the warm-ups and games, use the poster, sides 1 and 2, to introduce students to six key fitness elements that are part of a well-rounded workout.

Side 1 features six in-class fitness breaks from Section 2 that highlight each fitness element. You may want to hang it in an uncluttered corner of the room where students can go to take a quick fitness break on their own. Other useful places to hang the poster are by the gym or on the door heading outside to recess, as a visual reminder of what to notice or integrate into their physical activity.

Use the teaching guide on side 2 of the poster to learn more about the Super 6 and how to integrate these terms and concepts into your curriculum.

Side 1: Warm-ups and definitions for students

Side 2: Teaching guide with activities and curriculum connections

THE SUPER 6 FITNESS ELEMENTS

 Agility: skillfully moving through a series of precise movements

 Coordination: controlling movements in a synchronized way

 Flexibility: ability to stretch muscles and open joints fully

 Mobility: being in constant motion

 Stability: having control and balance when holding a position or moving

 Strength: using energy in the muscles to hold or move weight

To help students identify each element and begin to explore their own fitness habits, have them fill in a copy of My *Super Fit Page* (page 63).

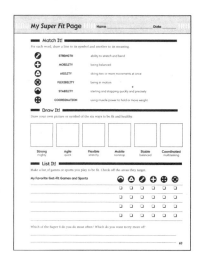

Cat, Cow

Mobilize your spine.

FLEXIBILITY   MOBILITY   STABILITY | **1 MINUTE**

1 Come down to the floor on your hands and knees. Put your hands under your shoulders and your knees under your hips, like a table. Breathe in.

2 Arch your back high like an angry cat. Try to reach your nose to your belly. As you move, let out a long hiss.

3 Let your belly get heavy and slowly drop until it hangs low, like a cow's belly. Raise your head to catch a breeze with your nose. As you move, breathe in deeply.

TIP!   Imagine your belly full of tasty grass. Moo!

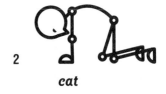

1

2
cat

3
cow

4 Repeat cat and cow five times slowly, five times quickly, and five times slowly again. Change with each breath in (cow) and breath out (cat). Try to move smoothly, without stopping.

Diamond-Legs Stretch

Stretch your legs and treat them like gems!

FLEXIBILITY MOBILITY | **1 MINUTE**

1 Sit on the floor with your legs extended in front of you and reach for your toes.

1

> **TIP!** Don't stretch too far. If your body's saying "ouch!" start over. Reach only until you feel warmth in the backs of your legs.

2 Pull your feet in until the soles are touching and you can hold them together with both hands. Your legs will form a diamond shape.

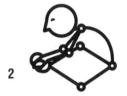
2

3 Hold your feet in place and scoot or slide your bottom up toward your heels, making the diamond shorter and wider. Stop when you feel a warm stretch from your knees to your hips.

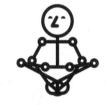
3

> **TIP!** Let your head float above your shoulders.

4 Hold your feet in place and scoot or slide your bottom back until you feel a warm stretch from your toes to your knees.

4

5 Release your feet, lengthen your legs, and try steps 1 to 4 again.

Dolphin Dive

Swim through the air to mobilize your spine!

FLEXIBILITY MOBILITY | 1–2 MINUTES

1 Standing up, join your hands over your head to make a long dolphin beak. "Dive" in these directions:

- Down, aiming for your toes—Dive deep! (flex)

- Up, aiming for the wall behind you—Begin a backflip! (extend)

- Left (side bend)—Take a sharp turn!

- Right (side bend)—Take a sharp turn the other way!

- Around the back left—Look out for sharks behind you! (rotate)

- Around the back right—Look out for sharks behind you the other way! (rotate)

- Upward in a wave—Do a dolphin wiggle! (undulate)

TIP! Look in each direction as you dive!

2 Try these moves in a smooth sequence: down, up, side to side, rotating left and right, and in a wave. Try the sequence five times.

3 "Swim" around your desk area using all of these moves.

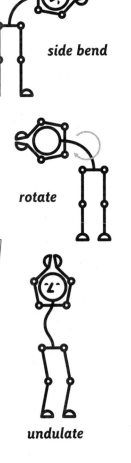

1

flex

extend

side bend

rotate

undulate

Down Dog With a Lift

FLEXIBILITY STRENGTH STABILITY | 1 MINUTE

*Can you balance upside down
with one leg lifted?*

1 Come down to the floor on your hands and knees. Start
in a table position, hands under your shoulders, knees under
your hips.

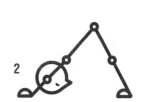
1

2 Take a deep breath. As you breathe out, push against the
floor with your hands and feet and lift your tailbone high.

3 Pedal your feet (alternate pressing one heel down and
lifting the other heel up) for ten counts to stretch
the backs of your legs.

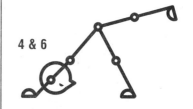
2

4 Keeping your arms and legs straight, lift one leg high.

TIP! Reach with your heel
to the sky!

4 & 6

5 Hold it for five to ten counts.

6 Switch legs and hold the other leg in
the air for five to ten counts.

7 Bring both feet down and repeat
steps 1 to 6.

Challenge: *Can you hold each leg
up for 20 counts? Longer?*

Figure 8s

Keep your 8s flowing.

COORDINATION MOBILITY STABILITY | 2–3 MINUTES

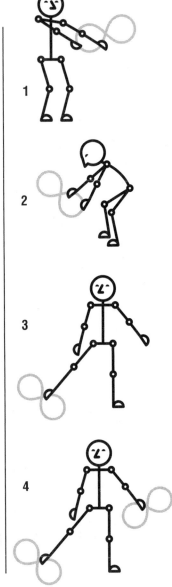

1 With long arms, make figure 8s all around you, low and high. Make a flowing stream of 8s.

2 Continue drawing ten more figure 8s, from your ankles to your heads, all connected. Try it fast and then slow. How small and large can you make the stream of 8s?

3 One at a time, use each big toe to draw figure 8s on the floor. If you can balance, stand on one leg and draw figure 8s in the air with the other. Try it for 30 seconds on each side.

TIP! The higher you lift your foot, the more balance you'll need!

4 Make figure 8s with an arm and leg at the same time. Try figure 8s with an arm and a leg on the same side and then on the opposite side.

Challenge: *Use other parts of your body to make figure 8s. What can you use to "draw"—your nose? hips? knees? ankles? Can you draw figure 8s in the air with each foot while sitting on the floor?*

Math Bonus! *What other numbers can you draw in the air that cross the midline of your body?*

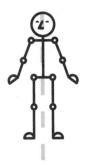

midline

Classroom Fitness Breaks to Help Kids Focus © 2011 by Sarah Longhi, Scholastic Teaching Resources

Fly-Catch Jumps

Jump like a hungry frog. Don't fall off your lily pad when you land!

AGILITY   STRENGTH | 1 MINUTE

1 Squat down like a frog and look up above, as if you're waiting for a fly.

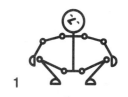
1

2 Count to three. Then jump up suddenly, clapping your hands above your head to catch a fly.

TIP! Your arms are like a frog's tongue!

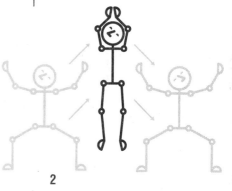
2

3 Come right back down to a squat. Hold your position until the next fly comes.

TIP! On your jump, try make your feet leave the ground and come right back to a balanced froggy-squat. If you lose your balance, make your jump lower until you feel steady. Then try it a little higher.

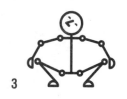
3

4 Try to catch at least nine more flies!

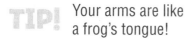

Vocabulary Bonus! *Can you show the difference between a jump, a hop, and a leap? Pay attention to how your legs push you up off the ground as you do each one.*

Freeze and Thaw

Hold a pose like an ice sculpture, then melt away.

STABILITY MOBILITY AGILITY | 1 MINUTE

1 Walk in place as you slowly count to 5.

2 Freeze on "5" and hold steady for at least five counts.

3 Now thaw: Relax all your muscles and melt to the floor like ice cream in the sun. Slowly count to 5.

4 Hop up and do steps 1 to 3 again. Freeze in a new way.

5 Try that three more times.

Thawing

Challenge! *Try step 1 with other movements you can do in place: marching, hopping, twisting side to side, turning in a circle, imaginary skateboarding, or your own move!*

Classroom Fitness Breaks to Help Kids Focus © 2011 by Sarah Longhi, Scholastic Teaching Resources

Glued-Feet Stretch

How far can you reach without coming unglued?

FLEXIBILITY STRENGTH STABILITY | 1–5 MINUTES

1 Stand with your feet and legs together.

2 Imagine there's a giant bubble around you. Use your arms to push the bubble away from every part of your body. Reach as far as you can in these directions:

a to the sides

b to the back

c to the front

d above you

e around the floor

 Are you sure you reached as far as you could around your feet? Try "ungluing" just your heels and walking out your hands on the floor.

3 Try pushing the bubble while you stand in a wider stance with your feet glued or while you sit with your bottom glued. What happens to the size of your bubble?

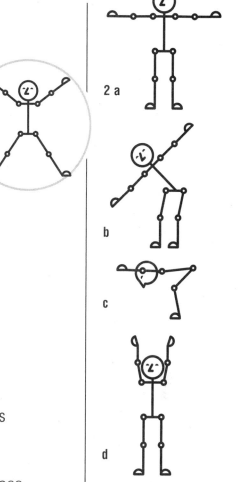

2 a

b

c

d

e

Math Bonus! *Can you reach in a complete circle (360 degrees) around the floor? What other geometric shapes can you create in the space around you?*

Heart Pumper

Make your moves big and stay in motion to give your heart some exercise.

AGILITY   MOBILITY   COORDINATION | 1–5 MINUTES

1 Run in place, pulling your knees up as high as you can. Count down, "Ten, nine, eight, seven. . . ."

2 Do 10 jumping jacks. Count down from 10.

3 Feet wide apart, alternate your arms, touching each hand to your opposite ankle. Count down from 10.

4 Walk your hands out on the floor until you make a long, straight line from your heels to the top of your head (plank position). Run your feet in place. Count down from 10.

5 Repeat steps 1 to 4 five to ten times.

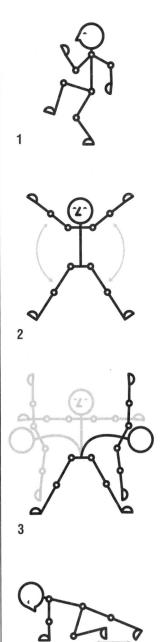

1

2

3

4

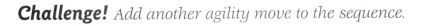

Challenge! *Add another agility move to the sequence.*

In, Forward, Up . . . Down, Back, Out!

AGILITY   COORDINATION   STRENGTH | **1 MINUTE**

Energetically jump to the right spot for each step.

1 Get in plank position and set your legs wide.

2 Jump your feet together. Say, "In!"

3 Jump forward, toward your hands. Say, "Forward!"

4 Pop up like an Olympic gymnast, arms lifted. Say, "Up!"

5 Drop down to crouching with your hands on the floor.
    Say, "Down!"

6 Jump back to plank position, feet together. Say, "Back!"

7 Jump your feet out wide, holding plank position. Say, "Out!"

8 Repeat the sequence 10 times.

*Jumping from
"Down" to "Back"
(Steps 5 and 6)*

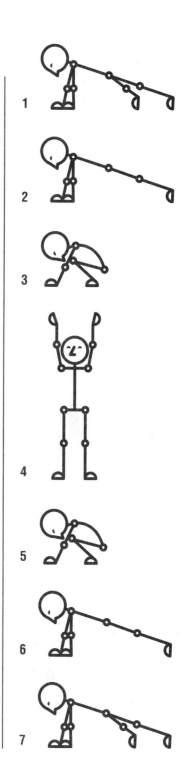

Classroom Fitness Breaks to Help Kids Focus © 2011 by Sarah Longhi, Scholastic Teaching Resources

Jump Around the Clock

STABILITY   AGILITY   MOBILITY | **2–5 MINUTES**

Try new jumping patterns with a clock face under your feet.

1   Stand, feet together, in the center of an imaginary clock on the floor.

2   Jump from the center to these points on the clock, each time returning to center: 12 ➨ 3 ➨ 6 ➨ 9. Count as you go: "Twelve, center, three, center, six, center, nine, center."

TIP!   You are moving clockwise.

3   Now move in the opposite direction: counterclockwise. Jump to each number starting with 12 o'clock without jumping back to the center. Count down as you go: "Twelve, eleven, ten, nine. . . ."

4   Make your own pattern with the numbers on the clock and repeat it several times. You might try these patterns:

6 ➨ 3 ➨ 9 ➨ 6   3 ➨ 12 ➨ 3 ➨ 12

6 ➨ 12 ➨ 6 ➨ 12 ➨ 9   4 ➨ 5 ➨ 6 ➨ 12 ➨ 11 ➨ 10

TIP!   Try your pattern, sometimes coming to center between each number and sometimes skipping the center.

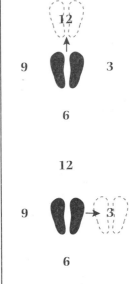

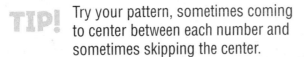

Math Bonus! *Imagine the clock is two-legs long in diameter. Crouch in the center of the clock and use one leg stretched long to be the minute hand and one leg tucked in to be the hour hand. Use different ways of stretching and reaching your legs to show the time now, in one hour, in one half hour, two hours ago. Make up your own time and see if a classmate can guess it.*

Classroom Fitness Breaks to Help Kids Focus © 2011 by Sarah Longhi, Scholastic Teaching Resources

Mashing Potatoes

Letting your fingers get in the action is great exercise for your arms.

MOBILITY STABILITY AGILITY | 1 MINUTE

 TIP! Do each movement to a count of 15.

1. Dig! Kneeling, use your hands to dig up as many potatoes as you can.

2. Chop! Use the edges of your hands like blades to chop up the potatoes. Chop as quickly as you can.

3. Stir! Standing, use both hands to stir your potatoes in a giant pot. Stir in both directions.

4. Mash! Mash the potatoes vigorously, lifting the masher up and down with both hands.

5. Repeat the sequence three more times without stopping.

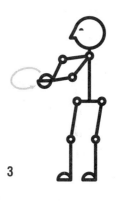

Mouse, Frog, Cat, Dog

Give your back a stretch break—
you've probably been sitting a while!

FLEXIBILITY MOBILITY | 1 MINUTE

1   Sit with your arms wrapped around your knees, feet on the floor. Tuck in your head like a frightened mouse. Take three deep breaths.

1

2   Come forward onto your feet in a frog-like squat. Let your tailbone hang. If needed, place your fingertips on the floor for balance. Take three deep breaths.

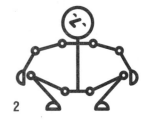

2

3   Gently roll forward until you're kneeling on the floor. Reach one hand forward like a stretching cat. Rest your forehead on the back of the other hand. Then switch hands. Take three deep breaths for each stretch.

3

TIP!   Imagine you're sharpening your cat claws!

4   Push down on the floor with your hands and feet, lifting your tailbone high in the air. Take three deep breaths.

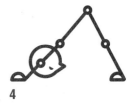

4

TIP!   Imagine you are a dog ready to play! You have an enormous tail that can touch the ceiling when you lift it up.

5   Try the sequence (mouse-frog-cat-dog) five more times, breathing deeply with each stretch.

Popcorn

Pop with speed and
stop with precision.

MOBILITY   AGILITY | 1 MINUTE

1 Tuck into a low squat, like a popcorn kernel. Imagine that you've gotten so hot, you have to pop.

2 Count to three and then jump to standing as if you're bursting open, legs and arms wide. Call out, "Pop!"

3 Hold the "pop" pose for a second.

4 Then come right back down into a tucked kernel squat. Call out, "Corn!"

5 Repeat steps 1 to 4, popping open into different shapes 20 to 30 times.

1

2 & 3

4

Pretzel Twists

How twisty can you get?

FLEXIBILITY STABILITY | **1 MINUTE**

1 Stand or sit tall.

2 Twist yourself into a pretzel, reaching your hands (and feet, if possible) around your body. Take three deep breaths.

> **TIP!** Try to wind yourself into different spaces, such as under your arms and between your knees. How small can you make yourself?

3 As you breathe out on the third breath, slowly unwind until you're back to standing or sitting.

4 Make at least two more different pretzels. Hold each one for three deep breaths and then unwind slowly.

1

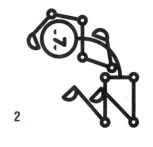

2

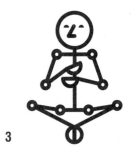

3

4

Push Up and Over

Build your arm power!

STRENGTH　STABILITY　| 1 MINUTE

1 Sit on the floor with your legs tucked to one side.

2 Using the strength of your arms, slowly lower your chest and head to the side opposite your legs. Your nose should be about one inch above the floor. Keep your legs together and let your feet come up off the floor.

1

3 Push back up, keeping your legs tucked in, and balance on your bottom. (Wrap your arms around your legs to help you stay steady.) Balance like this for a deep breath.

2

> **TIP!** Keep your toes on the floor for balance. Keep them off the floor to challenge yourself.

3

4 Lower yourself down to the other side slowly. Keep your legs together and feet off the floor.

4

5 Repeat the move as many times as you can in one minute.

Math Bonus! *If a complete move side-to-side takes about 10 seconds, estimate how many you could do in 2 minutes.*

Rubber-Band Arms

Get stretchy, breathe deeply!

FLEXIBILITY   MOBILITY | 1 MINUTE

1   Stand up tall at your desk. Take a deep breath in.

2   Interlace your fingers and push your palms away from your chest. Feel your shoulders open. Let a deep breath out.

3   Keep your arms extended and let go of your hands. Circle your arms around until your hands meet behind you.

4   Take a deep breath in as you interlace your fingers behind your back. Pull your chest away from your hands. Feel your chest open.

5   Repeat the two stretches slowly and smoothly, circling your arms to the front and back. Let your breath out as you circle and reach forward. Take a deep breath in as you circle and reach back.

. . . .

Challenge: *Lean forward as you reach back to stretch your legs and back.*

Scrape, Rumble & Jump

Scrape and stomp your hooves to let off some steam.

MOBILITY STABILITY AGILITY | **1 MINUTE**

1 Standing beside your desk, scrape each foot on the ground five times like a mad bull. Imagine sending a cloud of dust behind you.

> **TIP!** Hold the edge of a desk if you feel off-balance.

1

2 Drum your feet fast on the floor. Make it sound like a stampede is coming! Count down from 20.

2

3 On "One!" jump your feet wide and stab the air with your fingers pointing like sharp horns.

4 Try the sequence five times without stopping.

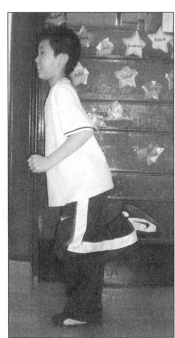

3

••••••••••••••••••••••••••••

Challenge: *Add 30 jumping jacks to each set.*

Seed-to-Root /
Seed-to-Sprout

STRENGTH FLEXIBILITY MOBILITY | **1 MINUTE**

Crawl out for water;
push up for sunlight.

1 Squat low and tuck yourself in a ball. Make a seed shape.

2 Walk your hands out on the floor to plank position.

> **TIP!** Imagine your hands as roots reaching into the ground.

3 Walk your hands in and tuck into a seed shape again.

4 With your hands pointing the way up, "sprout," rising like a new green shoot seeking the sun.

5 Repeat the rooting and sprouting, facing a new direction each time so that you cover the floor space around you in every direction.

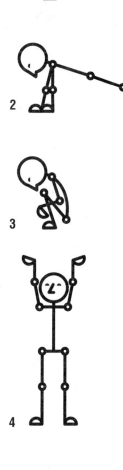

sprout

root

seed

Classroom Fitness Breaks to Help Kids Focus © 2011 by Sarah Longhi, Scholastic Teaching Resources

Shake It Up

Make some good vibrations
to wake up your joints and muscles.

MOBILITY	STABILITY	COORDINATION	1–2 MINUTES

1 Standing up, set your hands in motion. Imagine trying to shake water off of them.

2 Let the vibration move up into your arm and shoulders.

3 See if you can spread the vibration to your chest, legs, and finally your head so that your whole body is shaking like a wet dog.

4 Jump in place three times, saying "ha-ha-ha!" to get focused again.

5 Try steps 1 to 3 again and then stop moving one part at a time (head, chest, legs, arms, hands) until you are standing still.

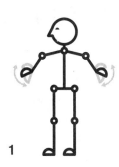

1

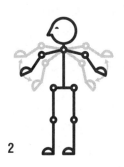

2

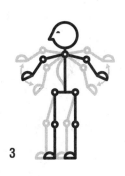

3

4

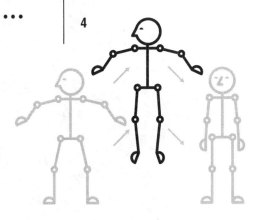

Challenge: *Shake two or three different body parts at once (for example, your right hand and left foot, left arm and left leg, or hips, chest, and head.)*

Sit Down, Stand Up— No Hands!

STRENGTH   MOBILITY   FLEXIBILITY   COORDINATION | **1 MINUTE**

Can your legs and core do it without help from your hands?

1   Stand tall.

2   Use your leg and core (belly and back) muscles to lower yourself to one knee.

> **TIP!** Keep your hands off the floor!
> Bend at your knees and hips!

3   Sit with your bottom on the ground.

4   Rise to standing again without using your hands on the floor.

> **TIP!** Look up as you rise.
> Push with your legs!

5   See how many times you can do sit-down-stand-up in one minute.

1

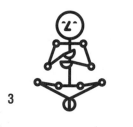

2

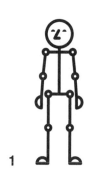

3

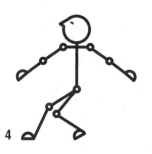

4

Skywriting With Your Toes

STRENGTH   MOBILITY   STABILITY | 1–2 MINUTES

How well can your toes and legs write?

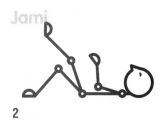

Jami

1   Sit on the ground or lie on your back with one foot on the floor.

2   Use the leg in the air like a giant pencil. Direct your toes to write the letters of your name.

2

TIP!   Keep the letters small at first.

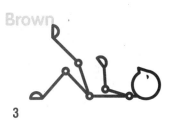

Brown

3   Switch legs and "skywrite" your last name. Is that side easier or harder to control?

3

4   Take a rest, hugging your legs to your chest. Then try a friend's name or the name of your pet. Can you write a full sentence?

4

Challenge: *Try skywriting with both feet together.*

Vocabulary Bonus! Ambidextrous *means being able to use both sides (hands or feet) equally well. Are you ambidextrous with your feet or is one leg easier to direct than the other?*

Soar and Rise

How far can you lift yourself off the ground?

STRENGTH   FLEXIBILITY | 1 MINUTE

1   Lie facing down on the floor. Rest your forehead on the backs of your hands.

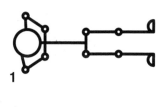

2   Lift your head and chest, looking straight ahead. Spread your arms like wings and lift your feet up like a tail. Hold and tweet 10 times.

> **TIP!** Imagine you are flying. See if you can lift all your ribs off the floor.

3   Move your hands under each shoulder. Tuck in your elbows.

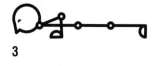

4   Push down on the floor with your hands and rise up like a snake, lifting your head and chest about a foot off the ground. Hiss 10 times.

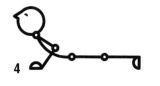

5   Come back to rest for a deep breath. Try soar-and-rise nine more times. Each time, hold the position one count (tweet or hiss) less.

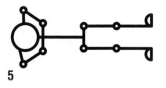

Space Walking

Imagine moving without gravity to hold you down!

STABILITY   STRENGTH   MOBILITY   COORDINATION | 1–2 MINUTES

1 Lie on your back. Imagine you're an astronaut with little gravity to pull you down. Practice floating all around without touching your feet or hands to the floor.

2 Try these moves on your back in slow motion:

> **TIP!** In space, each movement takes more time to do. How slow can you go?

a Let your feet walk all around in the air, as if you're stepping on the moon.

b Brush away space dust floating by your head.

c Roll to the side and move your legs as if taking 10 giant leaps one way. Roll to the other side and take 10 giant leaps back.

d Make a moon dust angel as you would a snow angel.

3 Try two or three more moves you would do on Earth, but slowly (for example, cycling, climbing a ladder, swimming).

Challenge: *Show how your moves would look to someone watching a video of your space walking in fast-forward or rewind.*

Section 2 **37**

Speedy Turns

How exact can you make each turn?

AGILITY   COORDINATION   MOBILITY   STABILITY | 1 MINUTE

1 Standing in the center of an imaginary clock under your feet, point your toes forward to 12 o'clock.

2 In one jump, turn to face the right side (3 o'clock). Make three more quarter-turn jumps (to face the back—6 o'clock, left side—9 o'clock, and front again—12 o'clock).

TIP! You are moving clockwise.

3 Now try a half-turn, jumping to face the back and then the front again (12 o'clock, 6 o'clock, 12 o'clock).

4 Try your quarter turns and half turns going in the opposite direction (counterclockwise).

quarter turn

half turn

• •

Challenge: *In one jump, can you turn all the way around the clock? How about three-quarters? Try your jumps clockwise and counterclockwise.*

three-quarter turn

full turn

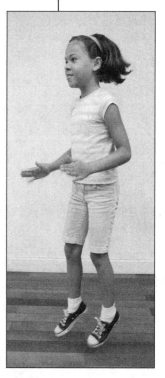

Classroom Fitness Breaks to Help Kids Focus © 2011 by Sarah Longhi, Scholastic Teaching Resources

Spread Your Wings

Fly like a slow-motion bird into a big stretch.

FLEXIBILITY COORDINATION STABILITY | **1 MINUTE**

TIP! For each step, breathe slowly on a count of five as you move.

1 Open your arms as wide as you can to catch the wind. Breathe in.

2 Push your arms together, still reaching long. Imagine slowly pressing the air out of a beach ball until your hands meet. Breathe out.

3 Bend at your waist, keeping your legs and arms straight. Breathe in.

4 Reach your arms way out to the sides, like giant eagle wings. Move side to side slowly, as if you're soaring above the clouds. Breathe out.

5 Pull your arms to your sides and reach far behind you. Reach forward with the top of your head, neck long. Breathe in.

6 Raise one foot, tucking it in to your body. Breathe out.

7 Lower the foot to the floor and rise up, spreading your wings and repeating the sequence. Breathe in.

8 Repeat this sequence five more times, changing the foot you raise in step 7 each time through.

• •

Challenge: *In step 6, extend your lifted leg, reaching it back to the wall behind you to look like a diving falcon.*

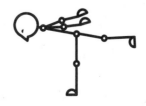

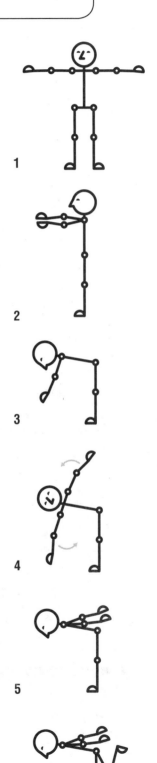

1

2

3

4

5

6

Taking Flight

Get your heart pumping with three kinds of wings.

MOBILITY COORDINATION | 1 MINUTE

1 Jog in place. Bring your knees up high.

2 As you jog, make these wing-like movements with your arms. Count to 10 for each:

a Flutter fast with back-and-forth pulses; keep your arms out to the sides, palms forward (hummingbird)

b Sweep your arms up overhead and back down to your sides (eagle)

c Flap short wings back and forth, elbows out to the sides (chicken)

3 Repeat the pattern or try a new pattern. Try out other types of wings.

TIP! What other birds do you know and how do they fly?

•••

Science Bonus! *Do an online search for smallest and largest wingspans. How do birds with very short and long wings move differently?*

1

2a

b

c

Classroom Fitness Breaks to Help Kids Focus © 2011 by Sarah Longhi, Scholastic Teaching Resources

Top-of-Your-Head Balancing

STABILITY · **MOBILITY** · **COORDINATION** | **1–2 MINUTES**

Can you keep an object balanced on your head while you move?

1 Find a light object with a flat side. Balance it on your head.

> **Examples:** a stack of index cards, a paperback book, a CD jewel case

2 Take three steps forward and then three steps back.

3 Find two different ways to sit down in a chair and stand back up again.

4 Touch the floor with your fingertips and stand back up again.

5 Slowly twist at your waist, turning right and left.

6 When you can do all these moves without dropping the object, make up your own challenging moves OR try the same moves with an object that's harder to balance, such as a pencil or paper cup.

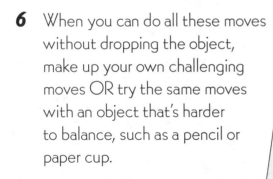

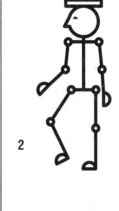
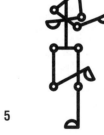

2

3

4

5

The exercises in this section fit right into your hallway transitions, whether you are moving or waiting. Encourage students to add their own variations and see if they can determine which of the Super 6 fitness elements they've incorporated.

· ·

TRAVELING TRANSITIONS

TRAVELING EXERCISES ADD 1–2 EXTRA MINUTES TO YOUR TRIP.

Creative Walks

MOBILITY   STABILITY   COORDINATION

Activate leg muscles and joints; develop core stability.

Inspired by a Monty Python sketch, this activity invites students to experiment with using leg muscles and joints in new ways to move forward. Encourage students to be creative—and laugh together.

NOTE: Remind students that their creative walk is never to serve as an imitation of someone with a disability. Their goal is to find new ways to move around the school.

1. Show students the four major joints that help us walk: hip, knee, ankle, ball of the foot. Explain that because each joint has a range of movement and can be coordinated with other joints, we can create a variety of ways to walk.

2. Demonstrate or have a volunteer demonstrate a unique walk for moving down the hall. This might include marching with knees lifting and arms swinging high, taking slow giant steps, kicking the heel of one foot with the toe of the other to hop forward, and so on. The possibilities are unlimited!

3. Alternate walking the usual way with creative walks (e.g., walk for 15 regular steps, then 15 funny steps, and so on). Arrive with smiles at your destination.

Science Bonus! As students move, ask them to compare the structure and range of movement of their leg joints with their arm joints (ankles and wrists, knees and elbows, hips and shoulders). How are these joints alike and different? Older students can explore an online visual dictionary to learn more about "types of synovial joints."

Doing a swivel step down the hall

Follow the Leader

Develop core stability, balance, and leg strength.

This simple walk-and-stop activity is perfect for hallway travel. Over the course of several days, let leaders rotate to allow all students a chance to lead.

1. Tell students you'll be the first leader as you all travel down the hallway. Stand at the front of the line, a few steps to the side, so that the whole line can see you.

2. Have students join you as you walk forward eight steps to a rhythmic count, such as "Walk, two, three, four, five, six, seven, eight."

3. Stop, freezing in midstep. With older, more physically confident students, choose a more challenging position, such as lifting and holding one knee high or balancing on tiptoes. Count out loud as you hold (e.g., "Hold, two, three, four, five, six, seven, eight.").

4. Repeat with variations (for example, add hopping, take a giant step, shuffle into the walking pattern: "Walk, two, three, four, hop, hop, shuffle. Hold two, three, four…").

Hopscotch Walk

Perform a quick, controlled pattern of hopping and jumping.

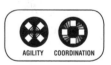

Interjecting a simple movement pattern during your walk down the hall gets kids focused instantly. Having students invent the pattern builds skills in sequencing as well as in agility and coordination.

1. Select or have students select simple moves inspired by (but not limited to) hopscotch to put in a pattern, such as the following:

- Jump your feet apart
- Jump forward, backward, or to the side (two feet at once)
- Hop forward, backward, or to the side (one foot at a time)
- Scissor-switching your legs while jumping
- Hold your balance on one foot to touch the ground
- Make a jumping turn in place

2. During a walk down the hall, announce "Hopscotch time!" Make sure students are a safe arm's length apart and then give them a countdown from 3 or another signal to begin together. Resume the walk and repeat again.

3. Make a class hopscotch-pattern-of-the-week: Give younger students two or three simple choices to put in a sequence. Have older students work out patterns on their own and introduce one each week to the class. Increase the challenge by trying the pattern backwards or working in a variation.

Writing Bonus! Hopscotch makes a perfect how-to topic. Have students create their own pattern, list the steps, and write an informative narrative paragraph. Post the how-to pieces in the hallway for other students to read and try.

Jumping a favorite pattern: Hop forward two steps, jump apart, jump and turn in place twice, hop forward and touch the ground. Then reverse it.

Skating Through the Halls

Use stability in the thighs and hips to move in a smooth pattern.

Students who are bursting with energy will exert as much energy "skating" as running, while also focusing on balance. Because "skating" can be done at slow to moderate speeds, it's great for moving through the hallways.

1. Have students put several feet of space between themselves and the person in front of them. (If the length of your line is a concern, then organize students in two parallel lines, staggering them so they are not right next to a classmate in the other line.)

2. Invite them to first "speed skate" in place by taking pushing-off steps from side to side.

TIP! Their free leg should come up and touch the inside of their opposite knee or thigh.

3. Once students are comfortable and can control the size of their steps, have them move forward with their steps, being mindful of the space around them.

4. Challenge students to add more momentum to their move by swinging their arms like a speed skater.

Twist and Walk

Improve coordination through varying walk patterns.

COORDINATION FLEXIBILITY MOBILITY STABILITY

Keep this walk slow to help students stretch their legs and focus; speed it up to emphasize coordination and balance and help students get extra energy out.

1. Have students form two lines, spacing themselves more than an arm's length apart.

2. Ask students to take a few steps in a straight line. Then tell them to imagine that their feet have magnets that are attracted to the floor on the opposite side. So whenever they take a step forward, they must cross in front of the other foot—a "pretzel step."

3. When they are comfortable and steady, make a game of alternating straight walking and pretzel walking (5 to 8 pretzel steps is a good number).

4. Increase the challenge by having students make figure 8s with their arms as they pretzel walk. First, have them cross their arms in the same direction as their legs. If they can do that, then have them cross their arms in the opposite direction as their legs. (This may take some practice!)

TIP! Suggest smaller steps to help students keep balanced and larger steps to add more challenge.

WAITING TRANSITIONS

WAITING EXERCISES TAKE ABOUT 1 MINUTE AND CAN BE REPEATED OR IMPROVISED ON TO FILL TIME.

Four-Sided Stretch

Lengthen shoulder and torso muscles.

This is a short and refreshing break that helps reorient students by having them turn 360 degrees to complete the move.

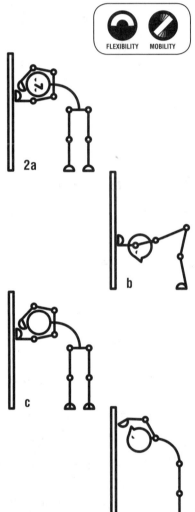

1. Have students form a single line, spacing themselves a full arm's length apart. They should be able to touch the wall with their arm fully extended to the side.

2. Have them try these moves in the following sequence:

   a Facing front, reach and press the hand closest to the wall into the wall and bring the other arm overhead. Lean toward the wall, keeping the pressing arm fully extended. Have them feel the spaces between their ribs opening up.

   b Facing the wall, keep legs and arms long. Bend at the waist until reaching the wall. Push palms against the wall and pull back with hips at the same time. Feel a stretch from your heels to your neck!

   c Facing the back of the line, repeat the first move, stretching the other side. Remember to keep pressing arm long and reach overhead toward the wall with the other hand.

   d Turning their backs to the wall, have them reach overhead for the wall behind. Let their fingertips touch the wall. If that feels like a big enough stretch, stop there. If students feel like they can keep going, walk fingers down the wall a few inches and then slowly walk back up and come to standing.

3. When students are familiar with each move, make this a 16-second break—count to 4 for each side they stretch. You can do three to four repetitions in a minute.

SAFETY TIP! For the back extension in step 2d, insist that students "walk" down the wall only as far as they can go and still come back up with ease. Their ability to extend back depends on the flexibility of their shoulders and spine and the length they have in the entire front of their bodies.

Froggy Up and Down

Build core and thigh muscles.

"Frog" squats build thigh strength and stretch hip flexors, making them a great break after long seated periods. (Yes, even older kids love moving like a frog!)

1. Have students form a single line.

2. Whenever the group comes to a stop, call out, "Froggy down!" Have students crouch down like a frog, bending deeply in the hips and knees and letting their tailbones drop toward the ground. They may either balance on the balls of their feet or, if they have the flexibility in their ankles and hips, squat on flat feet. If students are wobbly, encourage them to use their fingertips on the floor to help them balance.

FIT TIP! The more you have students stand up/ squat down (with little or no help from their hands and arms, of course), the more work they will do for their legs and core.

3. Call, "Froggy up!" to have them push up to standing (without using their hands). Have students who can do the move quickly and smoothly try balancing on the balls of their feet (on tiptoes).

Math Bonus! Make a game of assigning students numbers and calling specific numbers, or sets of numbers (e.g., odds or multiples of 2) to get different groups of students to squat ("froggy down") or stand ("froggy up").

The Great Partner Equalizer

Use equal force to perform coordinated movements with a partner.

This activity requires focused attention and physical cooperation between partners to balance together. The more partners pay attention to each other and make adjustments together, the more interesting and fun the shapes they make will be.

1. Have students line up by height so that when they turn to their partner, they will be facing someone who's about their height.

2. When you are stopped and waiting in the hallway, have students count off. Let the odd-numbered students turn and face the classmate behind them. Have partners press their palms together. See if students can really lean into one another without pushing too much one way or the other.

3. When partners have figured out how to apply equal pressure, have them try simple movements, like each lifting one knee and holding

it in the air, while maintaining their balance. Can partners stay connected as they squat down and get back up?

4. Ask students what they've learned about working with their partner. (Help students understand that the only way to move successfully and stay connected is by working together.)

Challenge! Older students can hold firmly to one another's wrists and pull away with equal force to sit down and stand up.

SAFETY TIP! Regulating force is a developing concept for children. You may need to have successful partners model the exercise for the class. Allow students to practice pushing "just the right amount" so neither partner pushes the other off balance.

One-Leg Waiting Stretch

Lengthen lower back and thigh muscles.

FLEXIBILITY   STABILITY

When students are lined up and waiting for the next class, the restroom, or the cafeteria, invite them to give their backs and thighs a break from standing.

1. Have students form a single line along a wall, spacing themselves a full arm's length apart.

2. Pressing one hand to the wall for balance, have them lift the opposite knee. Tell them to pull their knee gently to stretch their lower back. Have them turn around and switch legs to stretch the other side.

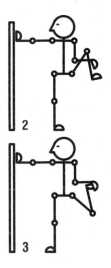

3. To stretch the fronts of their thighs, have students lift their heels toward their bottoms, keeping their bent knee pointing straight down. Encourage them to pull their ankle gently in by pulling on their sock, the heel of their shoe, or their pant leg. If students can do this without leaning and without discomfort, let them grasp and gently pull their ankle directly.

SAFETY TIP! Do not allow students to force their legs into a bent position—the connective tissues around the knees are sensitive and can be damaged when overstretched.

Wall Push-Ups

Build upper back and arm muscles.

1. Have students stand at least a foot away from the wall, facing it.

2. With both hands at shoulder height and keeping a straight line from head to ankle, have them do a push-up against the wall.

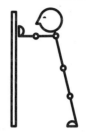

3. If this is too easy, add the following challenges. Have students do the push-ups in the following ways:

- One hand at a time, reaching up with the alternate hand (this shifts all the weight to one hand and adds an element of balance)

- With both hands, lifting one leg (this adds more weight to the push-up)

- One hand at a time, lifting one leg (this adds more weight and balance together)

FIT TIP! Make sure students use their palms and fingers to actively push into the wall. (This is excellent work for the fine-motor muscles of their hands and builds strength in their wrists.)

Challenge! Invite students who have mastered wall and traditional push-ups to try a vertical push-up—feet up on the wall and hands pushing up from the floor.

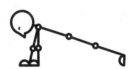

SAFETY TIP! Doing Wall Push-Ups allows students to use weight resistance to build upper-body strength without having to lift their full body weight, as in a traditional push-up. Once they have mastered the Wall Push-Up variations, let students try traditional push-ups. Make sure they can keep their bodies in a straight line, head to heel, as they lower and lift themselves.

The Wave

Activate the spine; develop timing.

FLEXIBILITY   MOBILITY   COORDINATION

A sports-spectator favorite, the wave is a fun way to reenergize the spine after students have been sitting or standing for a while. This move requires students to pay close attention to one another and make their timing precise so that their coordinated movement really looks like a seamless wave. This activity can also be done in the classroom as students stand in a circle or in two or three lines.

1. When students are waiting in line, have them turn to face you so they are standing shoulder to shoulder, a few inches apart.

2. On your signal and in one motion, the last student in line bends down and rolls up his or her spine with outstretched arms. When the student's arms have "crested" overhead, he or she releases them.

3. Just after this student has begun to roll up, the next student follows, moving through the same rolling wave motion and staying just behind the student who began.

4. Guide the wave down the line with each student following the next, about a second or two apart. (Note: The first few times, you may need to point to each student to cue him or her, so everyone can get a feel for the timing.)

Challenge! See how slow or fast students can make their wave and keep it smooth. Can they send multiple waves down the line or do the wave in reverse? What timing strategies can they use to help them stay together (e.g., counting beats or keeping their eyes on the person who moves just before them)?

Whole-Body Rock, Paper, Scissors

Change shapes in succession; develop core stability.

AGILITY   COORDINATION   STABILITY

A great way to help kids make decisions with a partner, this can also be done in the classroom, away from desks. In the hallway, it helps to boost concentration while you're waiting to move.

1. In a line, have students form partners (every other student may step out and face a partner in the original line).

2. Call out, "Three, two, one...rock! Three, two, one...paper! Three, two, one...scissors!" As you say the name of each tool, have students quickly take its shape. Here's how:

   • Rock: Tuck in low and tight to make a round rock shape.

   • Paper: Stand tall and reach your arms straight up beside your ears.

   • Scissors: Extend and scissor-switch your arms and legs twice.

Rock

3. Let partners play Whole-Body Rock, Paper, Scissors five to nine times to determine a winner. To start each round, tell partners to whisper-chant together with three jumps in place, "Rock, paper, scissors . . . Go!" On "Go," they must immediately take one of the shapes. The winning partner takes the shape of the more powerful tool: *Paper covers rock, rock crushes scissors, scissors cut paper.* In case of a tie, replay.

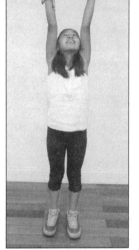

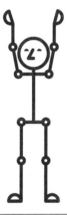

Paper

Rock versus scissors

Scissors

All the activities in this section are designed to involve the whole class in moderate to vigorous movement all at once. Invite students to add modifications that make the games more challenging. Emphasize that the goal is to stay active for at least 15 minutes at a time; challenge students to find ways to keep moving when they hit a slowdown.

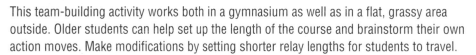

Action Relays

Complete movement combinations as quickly and accurately as possible.

MOBILITY   AGILITY   COORDINATION

This team-building activity works both in a gymnasium as well as in a flat, grassy area outside. Older students can help set up the length of the course and brainstorm their own action moves. Make modifications by setting shorter relay lengths for students to travel.

1. To prepare, set a starting/finish line and a return marker for each team. Determine the maximum number of teams that can race at the same time in the space you have (the more teams, the more opportunities each player has to participate and exercise). Organize students in groups of three to five.

2. Gather the class and lay down the ground rules. For example, team members must do the following:

- Perform the chosen move correctly.
- Touch the opposite wall or designated marker before returning.
- Do other exercises (e.g., jumping jacks) and cheer while they wait their turn.
- Sit down together as soon as their team has completed the race.

3. Choose or have the class brainstorm several fun actions they can do to make the relay challenging, but doable (e.g., skip and clap, log roll, and frog hop).

The action: Shoot toward an imaginary hoop or kick and touch your toes.

4. Walk students through the course of the race.

5. Have teammates line up in any order you or they choose (e.g., by height, alphabetical by first name).

6. Give your starting signal. The first team to have all players back in their original order, all doing jumping jacks together, gets to choose the action for the next race.

Vocabulary Bonus! Let students generate ideas for the relay by brainstorming and choosing from action verbs, such as *skip, jump, leap,* and *wiggle.* Challenge older students to come up with strong verbs, such as *scramble, creep, march, zoom,* and *gallop,* for their actions. Use these as vocabulary words for the week.

Boot-Camp Tag

Experiment with weight-resistance movements to build whole-body strength.

Letting students help choose the boot-camp exercises usually makes this game more challenging, but also more fun. A gym floor or smooth, paved outdoor surface works well.

TIP! If the "Its" are consistently having trouble tagging their peers, make the boundaries smaller.

1. Set boundaries within which all players must stay. (Let students determine a challenging activity for anyone who goes out of bounds, such as ten jumping jacks or five push-ups.)

2. Let two students start as "It." They must decide and announce what strength move their peers will do if tagged (they can choose from the moves they've learned in other activities or make some up on the spot). They must try to tag as many peers as possible in two minutes.

3. Set a signal (e.g., three claps, a whistle) that marks when the "Its" should rotate. When the signal sounds, let the current "Its" choose their successors.

Capture the Ball

Develop speed and accuracy in a series of short races.

In this fast-paced racing game, students challenge a new classmate each round in an attempt to earn points for their team.

1. In a large open space, mark a starting line in the middle and two tag lines at opposite ends, equidistant from the starting line.

2. Divide the class into two teams and have them line up, each team member on one side facing an opposing team member across the starting line. Explain that each pair of opposing teammates are "racing partners." Now have students stagger themselves along the starting line so that they are next to their racing partner, facing in the opposite

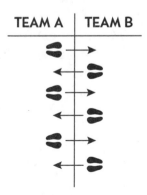

direction, and have an open space in front of them. (See Tip at right for working with an odd number of students.)

3. Place a small ball between each pair of racing partners. (In place of a ball, use any object that students can run with safely, such as wadded-up paper from the recycling bin.)

4. Explain the rules:

   • You will give a set of signals to start the race: On "Get ready," students crouch down. On "Get set," students reach one leg back in a low lunge or get down into a push-up position (more challenging). On "Go!" they shuttle themselves forward and the race begins.

   • Students must shuttle themselves forward to run to the tag line on the other side of the field, tag it, and race back to the ball.

   • The first racing partner to reach the ball grabs it and holds it in the air—captured!

   • The number of balls each team captures is the number of points each team earns. (Points will be tallied each round and added together for a final score.)

   • At the end of each round, players return to their sides and set the balls on the starting line. One team will rotate positions so that students have a new racing partner each round.

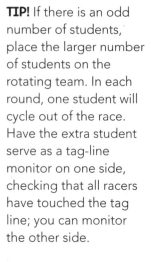

TIP! If there is an odd number of students, place the larger number of students on the rotating team. In each round, one student will cycle out of the race. Have the extra student serve as a tag-line monitor on one side, checking that all racers have touched the tag line; you can monitor the other side.

5. Have students walk through one round of the race to review the course and the rules. (Invite students to decide what will happen if a teammate does not tag the line—for example, one point is added to the opposing team's score for a missed tag.) Encourage a friendly attitude by having racing partners shake hands or high-five before rotating to the next partner.

6. Start the race. See if you can minimize the wait time between rounds so students will keep their heart rates up.

Math Bonus! At the end of each round, have students do mental math to add each team's score from the current round to its total. Back in the classroom, take the tally sheet and guide students to make a bar graph that represents the scores from each round. Have students analyze the results and write a set of questions for their graph.

Get ready.

Get set.

Go!

Circle-Me Relay

COORDINATION   MOBILITY   STABILITY

Build spatial awareness and teamwork skills.

You can make the race increasingly harder for students who master the basic course and are ready for a greater physical challenge.

1. Find a large open space that is wide enough for five to seven clusters of students to spread out across and is long enough for students to run at least 30 feet in one direction. Mark a starting line at one end and a line that teams must tag before they turn around at the other.

2. Organize students into teams of five or six. (Make sure all teams have an equal number of students. Have any teams short a member elect someone to take an additional turn.)

3. Explain the rules:

   • All the team members will run in each round of the relay. A round consists of running to the tag line and returning to the starting line.

   • Teams run together, forming a circle with their arms around one teammate in the middle.

   • Each time the team completes a round of the relay and returns to the starting line, a new team member gets a turn running in the middle of the group (i.e., teammate number 1 is in the middle first, then teammate number 2, and so on).

   • If a team's circle of hands is broken or if any team member touches the teammate in the middle, they must return to the starting line. Remind students that they want to be very careful to give the teammate in the middle of their group plenty of space and to work together to simultaneously move forward, stop, and return as smoothly as possible. (Encourage teammates to communicate with one another throughout the race.)

4. Have teams count off to determine the order in which each teammate will get a turn running in the middle of the circle.

5. Let teams try a walk-through of the course and have them note challenges, such as facing in different directions as the team moves together and having to adjust their speed to keep the circle together.

6. When teams are ready, give a starting signal to begin the race. The relay continues until each team has completed the course, with each of its members having had a turn in the middle. As soon as a team completes the course, have members sit down. Congratulate teams and discuss what it was like to work together, and encourage the fastest teams to share strategies they used to move together in a more synchronized way.

7. Rearrange teams and try the race again. You might invite students to add a challenge, such as having the teams do a series of moves (e.g., five jumping jacks or three frog jumps) at the tag line before they rejoin hands and return to the starting line.

Clean Our House!

Keep fully active, playing offense and defense at once.

MOBILITY   AGILITY   COORDINATION

This nonstop game is incredibly simple and full of fun. Use very soft foam or yarn balls 2 to 3 inches in diameter or even lightly balled-up paper from the recycling bin.

1. Use chalk, painter's tape, rubber discs, or other markers to evenly divide the game space. On the midline, spaced at least two feet apart, place eight to ten soft balls (larger groups may need more balls to keep the action moving).

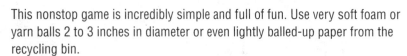

2. Split the class into two groups and set them on different sides of the midline.

3. Announce the rules:

- You must keep the balls out of your house (your side of the room/ space) by tossing back any balls that cross the midline; the object is to "tag" opposing team members with the balls when tossing them back.

- Tosses must be thrown underhand and stay low. Aim for legs and feet, never chests or heads.

- If you are hit below the waist or if you cross the line, you must go to the back of your house and do ten jumping jacks before rejoining your team.

4. Demonstrate the signal you'll use to call time and have students freeze (choose a clapping pattern, whistle, or other loud attention getter).

5. Start with a short round. (Stop the play if you need to review rules or safety tips.) When you call time, have each team count their balls and congratulate both teams: the house that's "clean" (fewer balls) and the one that's "messy" (more balls)!

Elastic Tag

Use familiar flexibility moves or invent new ones; use speed, stability, and coordination.

Inviting students to come up with their own "stretchy" moves encourages quick thinking and creativity as students try to avoid getting tagged.

1. Set boundaries within which all players must stay. (Let students determine a time-out activity for anyone who goes out of bounds, such as Cat-Cow or Pretzel Twists on pages 14 and 28, respectively.)

2. Let one student start as "It." He or she must try to tag as many peers as possible in two minutes.

3. When a player is tagged, he or she must stop and extend into a new or familiar position and hold the stretch. To be released, another player must come close and mirror that position for at least three seconds.

4. Set a signal (e.g., three claps or a whistle) that indicates when "Its" should rotate. When the signal sounds, let the current "It" choose a successor.

Freeze Dancing

Move to music; make and hold shapes during silences.

STABILITY   MOBILITY

This activity works in an open gym where students can spread out and dance, but it can also be done when they're in their seats with just their upper bodies dancing—in this case, "freezing" helps strengthen core muscles. Choose upbeat music!

1. Review the rules of freeze dancing:

   • While you hear the music, dance a safe distance from others unless you hear directions for a partner or group move, such as high-fiving.

   • When you hear the music stop, freeze immediately, holding the position you're in as best you can. (If you feel you will fall, make a small adjustment to stabilize yourself, such as bringing a lifted foot closer to the ground.)

   • Students who do not stop right away must hold their position until after the next freeze.

2. Do a test run by walking to music, and when students freeze the first time, help them find strategies for keeping their balance, such as holding their hands out and moving their feet into a wider stance.

   Challenge! When the music stops, call out a number from 1 to 4 (or 1 to 8 for older students). This is the number of body parts that must touch the ground as students freeze.

TIP! Some students, especially younger ones, will feel comfortable dancing on their own. You may want to give older students specific actions to do while the music is playing, such as skipping, galloping, walking backward, swimming, or skating (see page 44).

Get Up Off of That Foot!

STRENGTH MOBILITY STABILITY COORDINATION

Experiment with weight-resistance movements to build whole-body strength.

In this activity, a fun, high-energy song helps motivate students to experiment with creative, strength-building moves on the floor. Because of the floor work, this activity is best suited to a gym or stage. Make sure the floor is clean and free of splinters so that kids will feel free to crawl, slither, roll, and slide.

1. Make sure each student finds a place on the floor that's a full leg's length in all directions from others.

2. Ask students to take any seated or lying-down position, lift one foot off the ground, and hold it. Have them look around and notice all the different ways their peers are suspending their foot off the ground. (What's supporting the weight—arms, legs, core?) Now have them release the hold, shake out their limbs, and try lifting and holding the other foot in a different way. Encourage them to try the lift lying on their side, back, or belly—the more they experiment, the more fun they'll have—and the more exercise they'll get!

3. Explain the rules:

   • Move around on the floor in any way to the music (slither, slide, crawl, roll, squat-walk, etc.).

   • When you hear the chorus and the cue (the teacher will call out a body part), stop moving and lift that part off the floor. Hold the position until the verse comes and you can move around again.

4. Play a song students will enjoy that has a regular beat and frequent chorus, such as James Brown's "Get Up Offa That Thing." Just before each chorus, call out one of the following for students to hold up: right foot, left foot, belly, right arm, left arm, chest, bottom, both legs, both arms. Have them hold it up for the duration of the chorus.

5. If they need it, let students have a short break and then try it again. This time, students can choose the parts to hold up.

Go, Stop, Group!

Change locomotor patterns and change locations, keeping self-space.

Success in this game requires students to focus on oral directions, change their movement patterns efficiently, and negotiate space with peers effectively.

1. Use an open court or floor where you can randomly mark off spaces with chalk, painter's tape, or hula hoops. Make the spaces large enough for two to five students to stand in. (The number of spaces you'll need is equal to half the size of the group.)

2. Explain that this is a game that requires everyone to be extra careful about keeping their self-space: They will all need to move around in the same area quickly and in different directions.

3. Announce the rules:

   • When you hear the music, listen for the movement cue. Follow the directions and move all around the space.

   • When the music stops, freeze and listen for a number. That number tells you the size of the group that may fit in any of the marked-off spaces.

   • Move quickly to any space that has enough space for you and stand in it with your group.

   • If you do not find a group by the end of the countdown or if you touch anyone, you must move outside the game area and do jumping jacks or another fitness activity of your choice for one round.

Five can fit in this hula hoop.

4. Play the music and give a cue, such as crab walking, crawling, frog jumping, leaping, running, skipping, galloping, or any traveling activity students enjoy. Then stop the music, check that students have frozen and call out a number from 2 to 5. Give them a five- to ten-second countdown to find a group. Repeat.

Challenge! When students get to their group, have them hold a challenging pose, like balancing on one foot. Students who lose their balance must move outside the game area and hold a balancing pose for one round.

Math Bonus! On the ground, mark out larger shapes of geometric figures that students are learning. Call out directions that help them identify the shapes, such as, "Stand inside the rectangle or pentagon," "Stand in any shape except the square," or "Stand on the perimeter of the circle."

Quick-Change Moves

Change movement quickly and with control.

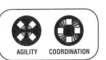
AGILITY COORDINATION

Use an open space in which students can suddenly change directions or gestures in response to a signal.

1. Select several loud sounds you will give to signal a quick change; pair the signals with an agility move, such as changing directions, Speedy Turns (page 38), Fly-Catch Jumps (page 19), or Popcorn (page 27). Examples of signals and quick-change moves might be:

- Clapping once: scissor-switch your legs four times.
- Calling "Turn!": make an immediate 90-degree turn (right or left) and keep moving.
- Calling "Fly!": squat and do a Fly-Catch Jump.
- Ringing a bell: do four Speedy Turns (quarter turns).

2. Try a few minutes of practice during which students walk around the space and respond to the signals without music. If students are ready for more of a challenge, start the music and have students dance or jog. Intermittently, give one of the signals and see how fast students make the change.

3. To increase the challenge, add more moves and give the signals in quicker succession.

Challenge! Ask students to notice which muscles and joints they can feel activating to help them make each change in their movement. Knowing where the action is coming from will help them become more aware and accurate in their movement.

Turn!

Hop or jump!

Red Light, Green Light

Use speed and balance control to move in a start-and-stop way toward your goal.

This old favorite tests how well students can regulate their movements.

1. Select a student to be the caller.

2. Have the rest of the class line up on a designated line at least 30 feet away.

3. Explain the rules:

- The goal is to be the first to tag the caller before he or she catches you.

- You may move only when the caller turns his or her back and yells, "Green light!"

- You must freeze in place when the caller yells, "Red light!" The caller turns to face the group immediately after yelling, "Red light!"

- The caller may point to you and tell you to go back to the starting line if he or she sees you move. (You can get caught for not stopping quickly enough or for moving during your freeze.)

4. Give students a dry run with you as the caller and ask the kids who are successful to share what they are doing (e.g., going at a slow or moderate speed that allows them to stop quickly or focusing all their energy on staying still when frozen).

Green light . . .

Red light !

My *Super Fit* Page

Match It!

For each word, draw a line to its symbol and another to its meaning.

STRENGTH — ability to stretch and bend

MOBILITY — being balanced

AGILITY — doing two or more movements at once

FLEXIBILITY — being in motion

STABILITY — starting and stopping quickly and precisely

COORDINATION — using muscle power to hold or move weight

Draw It!

Draw your own picture or symbol of the six ways to be fit and healthy.

Strong mighty | **Agile** quick | **Flexible** stretchy | **Mobile** nonstop | **Stable** balanced | **Coordinated** multitasking

List It!

Make a list of games or sports you play to be fit. Check off the areas they target.

My Favorite Get-Fit Games and Sports

Which of the Super 6 do you do most often? Which do you want to try more of?

ANSWERS FOR MY *SUPER FIT* PAGE

Match It!
Strength: using muscle power to hold or move weight; **Mobility:** being in motion;
Agility: starting and stopping quickly and precisely; **Flexibility:** ability to stretch and bend;
Stability: being balanced; **Coordination:** doing two or more movements at once

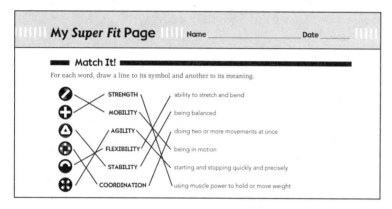

Answers for Draw It! and List It! will vary.

REFERENCES

Barros, R. M., Silver, E. J., & Stein, R. E. K. (2009). School recess and group classroom behavior. *Pediatrics, 123*(2): 431–436.

Centers for Disease Control and Prevention. (2010). *The association between school-based physical activity, including physical education, and academic performance.* Atlanta, GA: U.S. Department of Health and Human Services.

Ginsburg, K. R., & the Committee on Communications and the Committee on Psychosocial Aspects of Child and Family Health. (2009). The importance of play in promoting healthy child development and maintaining strong parent-child bonds. *Pediatrics, 119*(1): 182–191.

Ratey, J. (2008). *Spark: The revolutionary new science of exercise and the brain.* New York: Little, Brown and Company.

U.S. Department of Health and Human Services. (2008). Active children and adolescents. In *Physical activity guidelines for Americans.* Retrieval May 30, 2011, from http://www.health.gov/paguidelines.